You and
God
and Me
Together

P U B L I S H E R S
BOX 3566 · GRAND RAPIDS. MI 49501

PUBLISHING BOOKS THAT FEED
THE SOUL WITH THE WORD OF GOD.

You and God and Me Together

A Special Book for Parent and Teen

Exploring life, learning about our faith, and making the right moves

Jan Kempe

Nancy Munger, illustrator

LIBRARY OF CONGRESS CATALOGING-IN-PUBLICATION DATA
KEMPE, JANICE.
    YOU AND GOD AND ME TOGETHER : EXPLORING LIFE, LEARNING ABOUT
OUR FAITH, AND MAKING THE RIGHT MOVES : A SPECIAL BOOK FOR PARENT AND
TEEN / JAN KEMPE.
       P.   CM.
    INCLUDES BIBLIOGRAPHICAL REFERENCES AND INDEX.
    SUMMARY: APPLIES THE SCRIPTURES TO THE EVERYDAY DILEMMAS OF
CHRISTIAN TEENAGERS, ILLUSTRATING HOW OBEDIENCE TO GOD RESULTS IN
PEACE AND JOY.
      ISBN 0-929239-55-5 : $10.95
      1. TEENAGERS--RELIGIOUS LIFE. 2. FAMILY--RELIGIOUS LIFE.
3. CHRISTIAN LIFE--1960-   [1. CONDUCT OF LIFE. 2. CHRISTIAN LIFE.]
I. TITLE
BV4531.2.K45   1992
248.8'3--DC20   91-39183
                                        CIP
                                        AC

PRINTED IN THE UNITED STATES OF AMERICA

92 93 94 95 / CHG / 10 9 8 7 6 5 4 3 2 1

TO

MY LORD JESUS CHRIST,
WHO CAREFULLY PLANS THE LESSONS I NEED TO MAKE ME
MORE LIKE HIM

KRISTA, KEVIN, AND MIKEY,
WHO TEACH ME MANY OF THOSE LESSONS

JON, MY BEST FRIEND

F.E.W.I.C., FOR NAGGING ME IN PRAYER

CONTENTS

INTRODUCTION   8

CHAPTER   1   WHO SAYS THIS IS MY JOB,
              ANYWAY?   15

CHAPTER   2   I GIVE UP!   27

CHAPTER   3   SO, WHO'S GONNA KNOW?   39

CHAPTER   4   SAY, DID YOU HEAR ABOUT . . . ?   51

CHAPTER   5   I CAN'T BELIEVE MY LUCK!   63

CHAPTER   6   WHY? UH—BECAUSE . . .   75

CHAPTER   7   IT'S JUST NOT FAIR!   87

CHAPTER   8   LET'S PUT FIRST THINGS FIRST   99

CHAPTER   9   EXCUSE ME, GOD, BUT THERE
              SEEMS TO BE SOME MISTAKE   111

CHAPTER 10   IT'S HARD TO LET IT GO   123

CHAPTER 11   WHO CALLED ME?   135

CHAPTER 12   HE CAN'T BUG ME IF
              HE CAN'T FIND ME   147

INTRODUCTION

You and God and Me Together is not a book to give your teenager to use; it is a book to use with your teenager. To receive the most benefit, the two of you must sit down together and go through it page by page. Each chapter will bring you face to face with the kind of situations that come up in everyday life. Because neither of you is personally involved, however, you can discuss the situations openly and objectively. Questions are provided to guide your discussion, and a passage of Scripture is included to help you determine from God's Word the proper response.

The situations described are neither huge nor horrible. Instead, they are the small, everyday conflicts that bring to light questions concerning ethics and behavior. Each chapter begins with a story about an ethical dilemma. The pages that follow ask questions to get you talking about the dilemma, cite a similar incident involving Jesus, and encourage each of you to apply to your own lives the truth you learn from the biblical example.

The text is to be read aloud. Whenever you come to a question, stop and find out what each of you thinks. If you take turns reading and answering the questions, you will learn a lot about each other at the same time you are learning about God.

The purpose of the book is to help you work together to find the biblical answer to conflicts. An added benefit is that it will also help you learn to trust and appreciate each other's viewpoint on life's tricky situations. Agree ahead of time that your purpose is to seek God's guidance concerning troublesome situations and promise each other that you will never criticize or belittle the other person's opinion.

Before you get started, decide on a specific time to meet. Treat that time as you would a business appointment with your most important client. Use the calendars on pages 10–13 to plan your time together. Try to cover two sections per session, as the calendar blocks suggest. In session four, "Time Out" is an unstructured time that is just for fun. Use your own creativity to plan these times or follow the suggestions listed.

As you turn to Jesus for help in solving the problems presented here, you will be learning obedience to Him.

> Jesus replied, "If anyone loves me, he will obey
> my teaching. My Father will love him, and we
> will come to him and make our home with
> him."
>
> JOHN 14:23

MAKE A DATE

CHAPTER *1*	TIME/DATE	PLACE
1. STORY & QUESTIONS WHAT'S OUR EXAMPLE?		
2. WHAT'S THE ANSWER? BACK TO SQUARE ONE		
3. MOVING AHEAD KEEPING TRACK		
4. QUOTES & STUFF TIME OUT SMALL TALK		*Go out for pizza.* *The funniest thing I've seen someone do.*

CHAPTER *2*	TIME/DATE	PLACE
1. STORY & QUESTIONS WHAT'S OUR EXAMPLE?		
2. WHAT'S THE ANSWER? BACK TO SQUARE ONE		
3. MOVING AHEAD KEEPING TRACK		
4. QUOTES & STUFF TIME OUT SMALL TALK		*Attend a sports event.* *One thing I'd love to try someday.*

CHAPTER *3*	TIME/DATE	PLACE
1. STORY & QUESTIONS WHAT'S OUR EXAMPLE?		
2. WHAT'S THE ANSWER? BACK TO SQUARE ONE		
3. MOVING AHEAD KEEPING TRACK		
4. QUOTES & STUFF TIME OUT SMALL TALK		*Take a drive in the country.* *The funniest joke I ever heard.*

MAKE A DATE

Chapter 4	Time/Date	Place
1. Story & Questions What's Our Example?		
2. What's the Answer? Back to Square One		
3. Moving Ahead Keeping Track		
4. Quotes & Stuff Time Out Small Talk		*Go to the top of a high place.* *My dream vacation would be . . .*

Chapter 5	Time/Date	Place
1. Story & Questions What's Our Example?		
2. What's the Answer? Back to Square One		
3. Moving Ahead Keeping Track		
4. Quotes & Stuff Time Out Small Talk		*Surprise date! Parent's choice.* *The best thing I ever ate.*

Chapter 6	Time/Date	Place
1. Story & Questions What's Our Example?		
2. What's the Answer? Back to Square One		
3. Moving Ahead Keeping Track		
4. Quotes & Stuff Time Out Small Talk		*Go to a bookstore; look for funny books.* *A time I got laughing when I shouldn't have.*

MAKE A DATE

Chapter 7	Time/Date	Place
1. Story & Questions What's Our Example?		
2. What's the Answer? Back to Square One		
3. Moving Ahead Keeping Track		
4. Quotes & Stuff Time Out Small Talk		*Test drive a new car.* *If I had a million dollars . . .*

Chapter 8	Time/Date	Place
1. Story & Questions What's Our Example?		
2. What's the Answer? Back to Square One		
3. Moving Ahead Keeping Track		
4. Quotes & Stuff Time Out Small Talk		*Go to a mall and get ice cream.* *The most perfect place to live would be . . .*

Chapter 9	Time/Date	Place
1. Story & Questions What's Our Example?		
2. What's the Answer? Back to Square One		
3. Moving Ahead Keeping Track		
4. Quotes & Stuff Time Out Small Talk		*Surprise date! Teen's choice.* *The most scared I've ever been.*

MAKE A DATE

Chapter *10*	Time/Date	Place
1. Story & Questions What's Our Example?		
2. What's the Answer? Back to Square One		
3. Moving Ahead Keeping Track		
4. Quotes & Stuff Time Out Small Talk		*Go for a long walk.* *My most embarrassing moment.*

Chapter *11*	Time/Date	Place
1. Story & Questions What's Our Example?		
2. What's the Answer? Back to Square One		
3. Moving Ahead Keeping Track		
4. Quotes & Stuff Time Out Small Talk		*Find a quiet spot by water.* *My first childhood memory.*

Chapter *12*	Time/Date	Place
1. Story & Questions What's Our Example?		
2. What's the Answer? Back to Square One		
3. Moving Ahead Keeping Track		
4. Quotes & Stuff Time Out Small Talk		*Go to a park for a picnic.* *One thing I wish I would have done.*

ONE

Who Says This Is My Job, Anyway?

No servant is greater than his master, nor is a messenger greater than the one who sent him. Now that you know these things, you will be blessed if you do them.

LUKE 13:16–17

Andrew was in a hurry to get dressed and off to school, so he threw the covers up over his bed, stuffed the pile of dirty clothes into the hamper, and closed his bedroom door on the rest of the mess. Keeping things neat was such a pain!

As he gulped down the last bite of his breakfast he remembered that today was Wednesday. Garbage day. Great. The perfect way to top off a morning rush! Andrew wasn't sure how taking the garbage out to the curb came to be his responsibility, but it was.

Maybe just this once nobody will notice, he thought as he grabbed his book bag. "Bye Mom!" he called as he headed for the door.

"Have a good day, Andrew," his mother replied. "And don't forget the garbage. Today is Wednesday."

"It's not fair," Andrew mumbled as he lifted the last of the garbage bags and headed out to the curb. "This is the worst job in the house! Why do I have to do it every week? My allowance sure isn't enough to make up for all this aggravation! I don't see why Mom can't just do this herself instead of nagging me about it all the time!"

Andrew slammed the last brown bag down at the end of the driveway and it split wide open. Garbage splashed all over

the driveway and into the street. For a moment he just stood there and looked at the mess, then he knew just what to do. He raced back to the house, grabbed his book bag, and ran off to the bus stop before anyone could notice the mess and make him clean it up.

Discuss the following:

- Describe a time when you were in a situation like Andrew's.
- On a scale of 1 to 5, how would you rate the way you handled it?
- What things do you have to do that you think "shouldn't be your job?"
- Discuss how being a Christian should affect your attitude and behavior when you're asked to do something you think you shouldn't have to do.

Jesus was in a situation once where everyone said, "Hey, that's not my job!" Let's read about how He handled it and find out what we can learn about handling similar problems.

WHAT'S OUR EXAMPLE?

Take turns reading John 13:1–17.

¹It was just before the Passover Feast. Jesus knew that the time had come for him to leave this world and go to the Father. Having loved his own who were in the world, he now showed them the full extent of his love.

²The evening meal was being served, and the devil had already prompted Judas Iscariot, son of Simon, to betray Jesus. ³Jesus knew that the Father had put all things under his power, and that he had come from God and was returning to God; ⁴so he got up from the meal, took off his outer clothing, and wrapped a towel around his waist. ⁵After that, he poured water into a basin and began to wash his disciples' feet, drying them with the towel that was wrapped around him.

⁶He came to Simon Peter, who said to him, "Lord, are you going to wash my feet?"

⁷Jesus replied, "You do not realize now what I am doing, but later you will understand."

⁸"No," said Peter, "you shall never wash my feet."

Jesus answered, "Unless I wash you, you have no part with me."

⁹"Then, Lord," Simon Peter replied, "not just my feet but my hands and my head as well!"

¹⁰Jesus answered, "A person who has had a bath needs only to wash his feet; his whole body is clean. And you are clean, though not every one of you." ¹¹For he knew who was going to betray him, and that was why he said not every one was clean.

¹²When he had finished washing their feet, he put on his clothes and returned to his place. "Do you understand what I have done for you?" he asked them. ¹³"You call me 'Teacher' and 'Lord,' and rightly so, for that is what I am. ¹⁴Now that I, your Lord and Teacher, have washed your feet, you also should wash one another's feet. ¹⁵I have set you an example that you should do as I have done for you. ¹⁶I tell you the truth, no servant is greater than his master, nor is a messenger greater than the one who sent him. ¹⁷Now that you know these things, you will be blessed if you do them."

WHAT'S THE ANSWER?

In Jesus' day the most common means of transportation was walking, and sandals were the standard footwear. Travelers arrived at their destination with tired, sore, dirty feet. Roads weren't paved, so in dry weather feet got dusty and in rainy weather they got muddy.

Because of this, a custom developed. If you invited guests to your home, one of the first things you would do when they arrived would be to have your servant wash their tired, dirty feet in a basin of water.

When Jesus and the disciples arrived at the upper room, they had no wealthy host to greet them and no servant to wash their feet. Apparently none of the disciples felt like doing this lowly task—at least none of them volunteered—so they went ahead and started their meal, dirty feet and all.

While the meal was being served, Jesus got up from the table (v. 4) and got himself ready to wash feet. Notice that he didn't clear his throat and announce, "Well, if nobody else will wash feet, I guess I'll have to do it!" It was not Jesus' purpose to shame the others into embarrassment. That was not His style.

Imagine you were there. As Jesus came to you and loosened your sandals, what would you say? As He poured clean water over your smelly toes and gently wiped the day's dirt away, what do you think His attitude would be? As He finished wiping them dry and moved on to the next guy, how would you feel?

Discuss the thoughts that come to mind as you imagine yourself in this situation.

Look at verses 6–10. Good old Peter! Why was he embarrassed by what Jesus was doing? Why do you suppose he didn't volunteer to take over the dirty job and finish it for Jesus? When Jesus explained to him the importance of footwashing, Peter asked for a whole bath! (v. 9). Peter had a good heart. He wanted to obey Jesus, but he didn't always understand how to do it.

Nor do we. But we can learn if we pay attention to the lessons Jesus teaches us through His Word, through the lives of people in the Bible, and through the people around us.

BACK TO SQUARE ONE

Give some thought to Andrew's situation.

- What was the source of his aggravation?
- Now that you know how Jesus responded in similar circumstances, what new insights can you give Andrew?
- What would you suggest to make Wednesday mornings more bearable?
- What has the lesson about footwashing taught you about what Andrew's response should be?
- What about Andrew's mom? She has a couple of choices as to how to respond to this situation. What will you suggest? Has the lesson about footwashing taught you anything new about what her response might be?
- Discuss some ways to apply Jesus' lesson to this problem.
- Obedience to Jesus is supposed to bring happiness. How is that possible in this situation?
- If Jesus were to sit down with Andrew and his mom, what solution to the problem do you think the three of them would come up with?

MOVING AHEAD

Take some time to ask Jesus to show you ways to follow His example. Then discuss the following questions:

- Jesus washed the feet of His friends; what does that tell us about whom we are to serve?
- What are some ways we can follow this example now that footwashing is no longer done?
- What unpleasant jobs around your home does somebody else always get stuck doing?
- What chores don't get done at all because no one wants to do them?
- What could you do to make someone else feel loved and cared for?
- Determine to have a loving and pleasant attitude such as the one Jesus demonstrated.
- Decide whom you will serve and how you will do it.
- Keep a record of your thoughts and experience on the "Keeping Track" page.
- DECIDE: Is God's Word about footwashing true? (See v. 17.)

QUOTES & STUFF

Pride is tasteless, colorless, and sizeless, yet it is the hardest thing to swallow. —*August B. Black*

If you are too big to do little things, you are too little to do big things.

A highbrow is a person who has been educated beyond his intelligence.

One morning Thomas Jefferson woke up in a modest Washington rooming house, dressed, and then left the house in order to attend his inauguration as the third president. When he got back, duly sworn in, he found no space left for him at the dinner table. Quietly accepting the democratic principle of first come, first served, the President of the United States went up to his room without dinner.
—*The Little, Brown Book of Anecdotes*

JUST FOR FUN

Ohio is listed as the seventeenth state in the United States, but technically it is number forty-seven. Until August 7, 1973, Congress forgot to vote on a resolution to admit Ohio to the Union. —*The Bathroom Trivia Book*

KEEPING TRACK

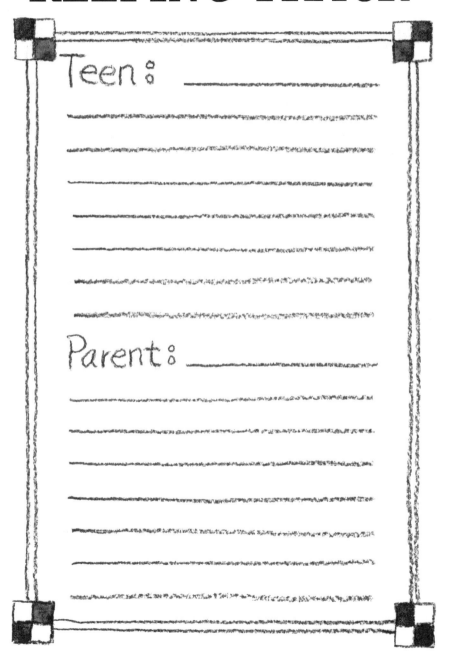

Teen: _____

_____

_____

_____

_____

_____

_____

Parent: _____

_____

_____

_____

_____

_____

_____

TWO

I Give Up!

They sat down in groups of hundreds and fifties. Taking the five loaves and the two fish and looking up to heaven, he gave thanks and broke the loaves. Then he gave them to his disciples to set before the people. He also divided the two fish among them all. They all ate and were satisfied.

MARK 6:40–42

T erry crumpled up her paper and tossed it into the growing pile in the corner of her room. "This just isn't going to work!" she sighed in frustration.

Terry's high school English department was having an essay contest on the topic *What really matters in life*, and Terry had volunteered to write the essay to represent her class. It seemed like such a good idea at the time! Terry and her family had spent two years on the mission field, but she always had a hard time helping her friends understand why they had done it. This seemed like a perfect opportunity to explain, but now the deadline was approaching and she couldn't get her words to come out right.

She tore another piece of paper out of her notebook and wrote the title on the top. "What really matters in life," she wrote, "is knowing the One who is in charge of it all." For a moment she seemed pleased with her sentence, but then she crumpled the paper and sent it flying across the room.

"I'm just not good enough," she mumbled. "Everybody can write better than I can. There's no way I can win. And if I write what I really believe, people will think I'm some sort of fanatic. And if I don't write it well enough, I'll make all Christians look really stupid."

Terry left her desk and flopped down on her bed. *Someone else should do this,* she thought. *I'm just not good enough.* A tear slipped out of the corner of her eye as she sighed another deep sigh. "My best just isn't good enough."

Discuss the following:

- Describe an occasion when you felt as if your best wasn't good enough. How did it turn out? What did you learn from it?
- If you were in a situation like this now, to whom would you go for help?
- How would you expect Terry's parent to react in this situation?
- How should knowing Jesus make a difference?

In the following story the only available answers seemed inadequate, and the disciples might have given up if Jesus hadn't stepped in.

WHAT'S YOUR EXAMPLE?

Take turns reading Mark 6:30–44.

³⁰The apostles gathered around Jesus and reported to him all they had done and taught. ³¹Then, because so many people were coming and going that they did not even have a chance to eat, he said to them, "Come with me by yourselves to a quiet place and get some rest."

³²So they went away by themselves in a boat to a solitary place. ³³But many who saw them leaving recognized them and ran on foot from all the towns and got there ahead of them. ³⁴When Jesus landed and saw a large crowd, he had compassion on them, because they were like sheep without a shepherd. So he began teaching them many things.

³⁵By this time it was late in the day, so his disciples came to him. "This is a remote place," they said, "and it's already very late. ³⁶Send the people away so they can go to the surrounding countryside and villages and buy themselves something to eat."

³⁷But he answered, "You give them something to eat."

They said to him, "That would take eight months of a man's wages! Are we to go and spend that much on bread and give it to them to eat?"

³⁸"How many loaves do you have?" he asked. "Go and see."

When they found out, they said, "Five—and two fish."

³⁹Then Jesus directed them to have all the people sit down in groups on the green grass. ⁴⁰So they sat down in groups of hundreds and fifties. ⁴¹Taking the five loaves and the two fish and looking up to heaven, he gave thanks and broke the loaves. Then he gave them to his disciples to set before the people. He also divided the two fish among them all. ⁴²They all ate and were satisfied, ⁴³and the disciples picked up twelve basketfuls of broken pieces of bread and fish. ⁴⁴The number of the men who had eaten was five thousand.

WHAT'S THE ANSWER?

This was an exciting time for the disciples. Jesus had sent them out in pairs to the surrounding villages to preach and teach. He also enabled them to perform miracles! Suddenly these ordinary men were able to heal the sick and cast out demons! (See Mark 6:13.) What do you think they might have been saying in verse 30?

Verse 31 says that people kept coming and going and the disciples and Jesus didn't even have time to eat. If word leaked out that someone in your town was doing miracles and healing the sick, what would happen? It caused such a commotion back then that Jesus decided they all needed a rest. A few days off would give the men time to unwind and try to understand all that had happened to them.

Verses 32–33 tell what happened to their plan. If you had been a disciple, how would you have reacted when you saw from the boat what was happening on the shore?

Jesus loved all the people. He wanted to tell them about God and His love, so He spent the rest of the day telling stories and healing those who were sick. The disciples were already tired and probably anxious for the crowd to go home, so how do you think they responded when Jesus told them to "give them something to eat" (v. 37)? How would you have responded?

The disciples were no longer thinking about miracles. Their focus was not on God's power but rather on their own

lack of it. They did as Jesus asked, however, and found one young boy who had brought his lunch, certainly not enough food to feed the crowd that covered the hillside.

They gave the lunch to Jesus, and He blessed it. Then He broke the bread and gave it to them to distribute. Jesus broke off more and more, and still it was not gone! Imagine what it must have been like to serve the broken pieces of bread and fish to everyone in sight and still have a full basket.

Read verses 42–43. Did everybody take just a little? Did they eat up every crumb? Keep in mind that the number 5,000 in verse 44 refers to men only. They didn't count women and children. When that small lunch was put into Jesus' hands, it was enough to feed everyone around. Jesus taught an important lesson that day. No matter what we have to offer, no matter how insignificant it may seem, Jesus can make it enough. Jesus can make it a feast for everyone around!

This miracle still happens when we give our gifts to Jesus.

BACK TO SQUARE ONE

Give some thought to Terry's situation.

- What was Terry's biggest fear?
- How does this lesson apply to her problem?
- What have you learned that might help her? What would you like to tell her?
- If Jesus were to sit down with Terry, what solution to the problem do you think the two of them would come up with?

In giving Terry some advice and encouragement, you may stumble on a gift you have to offer. Being an encourager is one way to be sure Jesus uses you frequently. Possibly the best encouragement we can give is to remind people of who Jesus is and what He asks of us.

MOVING AHEAD

Discuss what gift you have to offer. It may be obvious to you, or you may need to think about it for a while. Ask Jesus to give you a hint about where to find the answer. If you think your gift isn't good enough, consider what Jesus did with five hunks of bread and two smelly fish that had spent all day in the hands of a little boy in the hot sun—with no plastic wrap! And remember that it came from a little boy. Jesus will take whatever we give Him. He doesn't ask that we make it perfect first.

Jesus didn't always work with crowds. Most of His work was one on one. He may not bless a whole crowd with your gift, but it may be just the thing He can use to change one life.

- Identify a gift you are willing to give.
- Take it to Jesus and ask Him to make it a good gift.
- Watch expectantly for opportunities to use your gift to benefit those around you.
- Keep a record of your thoughts and experiences on the "Keeping Track" page.

QUOTES & STUFF

You are never a loser until you quit trying. —*Mike Ditka*

We are all faced with a series of great opportunities brilliantly disguised as impossible situations. —*Chuck Swindoll*

Be not simply good. Be good for something.
—*Henry David Thoreau*

God has not called me to be successful; he has called me to be faithful. —*Mother Theresa*

JUST FOR FUN

What do these things have in common?

Baby lotion, shampoo, wood stain, dye for cloth, caramel, chili sauce, dehydrated milk flakes, instant coffee, mayonnaise, sweet pickles, Worcestershire sauce, asparagus substitute, treatment for goiters, diesel fuel, charcoal, glue, insecticides, nitroglycerin, paper, plastics, rubber, laundry soap, and ink.

All of these and more than 250 additional products can be made from the peanut.

KEEPING TRACK

Teen: _____

_____

_____

_____

_____

_____

_____

Parent: _____

_____

_____

_____

_____

_____

_____

THREE

So Who's Gonna Know?

Man does not live on bread alone.

LUKE 4:4

Don Jansen left his desk and went out to the coffee machine where a few other employees had gathered for break. The discussion this afternoon was about the 15 cents per copy charge for all personal copies made on the company copy machines. Up until today employees had been able to make free copies for personal use.

Several of the employees made known their thoughts about the policy. They said they deserved better treatment! Don didn't say much. He realized that the new manager had the authority to enforce the policy, but it did seem kind of petty. The company offered so few fringe benefits!

As Don sat down at his desk again he spotted the publicity flyer he had volunteered to run off for his son's little league car wash. It could get expensive running those copies now.

Don worked late that evening, and on his way out he noticed the deserted copy machine. *It can't be that wrong to run this one batch,* he thought. *After all, the policy just started today. What if I had brought these in yesterday? What if I say I never got notice of the policy change? Who's to know?*

Discuss the following:

- Describe a time when you were in a situation like this. What happened? What did you learn from it?
- On a scale of 1 to 10, how big is this problem?
- What do you think is causing Don's problem here? After all, no one is looking.
- If Don's son had been with him, how might his thoughts have been different?
- How does being a Christian make a difference?

When temptation makes you feel conflict within yourself, pay attention to that uneasy feeling. Jesus didn't take temptation lightly. After this chapter you will be more aware of where temptation comes from and why Don needs someone to plunk a DANGER sign down on the copier.

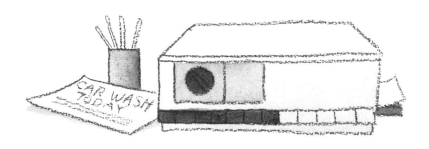

WHAT'S OUR EXAMPLE?

Take turns reading Luke 4:1–13.

¹Jesus, full of the Holy Spirit, returned from the Jordan and was led by the Spirit in the desert, ²where for forty days he was tempted by the devil. He ate nothing during those days, and at the end of them he was hungry.

³The devil said to him, "If you are the Son of God, tell this stone to become bread."

⁴Jesus answered, "It is written: 'Man does not live on bread alone.'"

⁵The devil led him up to a high place and showed him in an instant all the kingdoms of the world. ⁶And he said to him, "I will give you all their authority and splendor, for it has been given to me, and I can give it to anyone I want to. ⁷So if you worship me, it will all be yours."

⁸Jesus answered, "It is written: 'Worship the Lord your God and serve him only.'"

⁹The devil led him to Jerusalem and had him stand on the highest point of the temple. "If you are the Son of God," he said, "throw yourself down from here. ¹⁰For it is written:

> "'He will command his angels
> concerning you
> to guard you carefully;
> ¹¹they will lift you up in their hands,
> so that you will not strike your
> foot against a stone.'"

¹²Jesus answered, "It says: 'Do not put the Lord your God to the test.'"

¹³When the devil had finished all this tempting, he left him until an opportune time.

W<small>HAT'S</small> <small>THE</small> ANSWER?

This Scripture passage is so full of things we need to learn that this and the next two chapters will all come from it. Jesus went through the worst possible temptations and never gave in. To be like Him, we need to know where temptation comes from. Read verse 2 and identify the tempter.

To fast is to give up one thing and replace it with something else. We can give up food temporarily and replace it with prayer, or we can give up TV and replace it with Bible study for a time. Going without something does us no good unless we replace it with something more worthwhile. Why do you think Jesus went without food for forty days? What do you think He replaced it with?

Would it have been wrong for Jesus to make a stone into bread? Why? Can you think of a time when Jesus used His power to do something for Himself? Do you think He ever zapped up a quick, hot supper when He was hungry and no one was looking?

If Jesus had used His power to make life easy for Himself, it would have been no great accomplishment for Him to have lived a perfect life. His claim to have been perfect yet "fully human" would have been weakened if He had used "super-human" powers to accomplish it. This is very important because only a perfect sacrifice is acceptable to God, so a perfect human had to die to reconcile the human race to God. Jesus was fully God because He had the power of God, but He chose

44

to be fully man and not use that power to give Himself any personal advantage over other humans.

Everything He did on earth for Himself was done the way you and I do things. No magic. When He needed to lift something, He strained muscles. If He got hurt, He felt pain! The devil tempted Him over and over again to take the easy way out, but Jesus chose to use His power only to glorify His Father in heaven.

Read Hebrews 2:18. Who tempts us? Why? As Christians, we represent Jesus' physical presence on earth. We are the ones He has asked to spread His Gospel. How do you think Satan feels about this? What do you think he'd like to do about it?

One thing Satan is really good at is subtle temptation. So when thoughts like, *Well, it's not that wrong* go through your mind, remember that they come from the one who urged our hungry Savior to make Himself "just a little bread."

Through Jesus we have the power to overcome the devil if we learn to recognize him. It is wrong to let Satan have even a small victory in our lives.

BACK TO SQUARE ONE

Give some thought to Mr. Jansen's situation.

- What advice do you have for him? The Little League car wash is a good cause. No one will know if he makes the copies, so what will it hurt?
- Suppose that you are Mr. Jansen and there is nobody there to give you advice. If you feel the temptation taking over, what can you do to maintain control?
- If you make the copies, what will happen the next time a company policy is to your disadvantage? Will it be harder or easier for you to make the right choice?
- Obedience to Jesus' example is our goal. What would He do?
- If we choose to sin a little every now and then, how will it affect us?

When we recognize who temptation comes from the right choices come more easily.

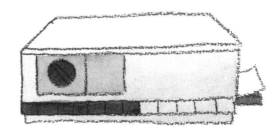

MOVING AHEAD

It would be easier for all of us to avoid temptation if the devil paraded around in red pajamas and carried a pitchfork so we could recognize him, but he doesn't. Matthew 4:3 calls the devil the tempter. The feminine form of this word is temptress, a person who uses beauty to entice a person to sin.

• What does that tell you about Satan?
• Keep a list for the next few days of things that tempt you and what the consequences might be of giving in to those temptations.
• Share what you have learned. God has given you each other to help you through situations like these.
• Even small temptations can lead us away from where God wants us to be. When you recognize one, give it up and replace it with God's promise in Hebrews 2:18.
• Keep a record of your thoughts and experiences on the "Keeping Track" page.

Jesus has won the battle with the devil, so we need not fear his power. We must be careful, however, not to be fooled by his disguises.

QUOTES & STUFF

Live so that your friends can defend you but never have to. —*Arnold H. Glasow*

A real Christian is an odd number, anyway. He feels supreme love for one whom he has never seen; talks familiarly every day to someone he cannot see; expects to go to heaven on the virtue of another; empties himself in order to be full; admits he is wrong so he can be declared right. Goes down in order to get up; is strongest when he is weakest, richest when he is poorest, and happiest when he feels the worst. He dies so he can live; forsakes in order to have; gives away so he can keep; sees the invisible, hears the inaudible, and knows that which passes knowledge. —*A. W. Tozer*

Unless you believe, you will not understand. —*Augustine*

JUST FOR FUN

The new employee stood before the paper shredder looking confused. "Need some help?"a secretary asked. "Yes," he replied. "How does this thing work?" "Simple," she said, taking the thick report from his hand and feeding it into the machine."Thanks," said the new employee. "Where do the copies come out?" —*Kermit Moore in American Way*

KEEPING TRACK

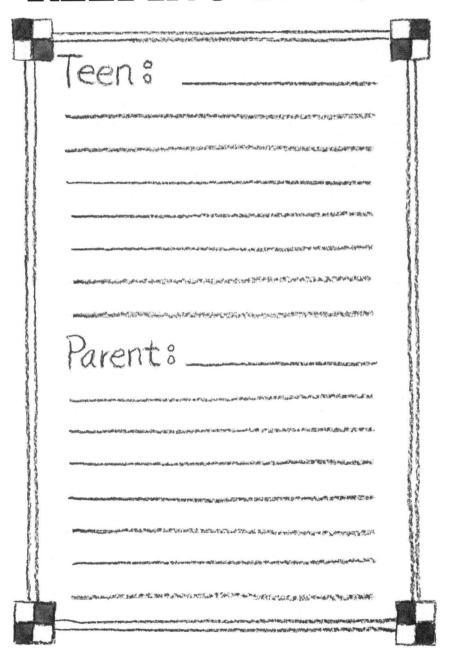

Teen: _____

_____

_____

_____

_____

_____

_____

_____

Parent: _____

_____

_____

_____

_____

_____

_____

_____

FOUR

Say, Did You Hear About . . . ?

Worship the Lord your God and serve him only.

LUKE 4:8

Susan and her husband had saved for years to be able to move into a nice section of town. Susan was eager to make friends with her new neighbors but she felt a little intimidated by the people she had seen on her street. They drove expensive cars and wore nice clothes even for jogging. Susan drove a twelve-year-old station wagon and preferred sweat pants and a T-shirt. Sometimes she wondered if any other houses on the street had unfurnished rooms like her living room.

Still, they had worked hard to live here and she was determined to develop some friendships.

One afternoon Susan received an invitation to a brunch for all the women on the block. Susan was worried that her clothes weren't right or that she'd say the wrong things, but her husband assured her that she would be just fine.

"Just be yourself," he called over his shoulder as he left for work.

Susan paid attention when she was introduced to the women so she could remember their names. Everyone seemed genuinely friendly and she was encouraged. Then the hostess made a remark about the women who had not come. As the conversation shifted, Susan began to feel uneasy. Everyone had

stories and jokes about the missing neighbors. Susan wanted so much to fit in! *If I just go along with this, they might accept me,* she thought. *I'd hate to get them talking about me behind my back! Besides, what will it hurt if I just don't say anything?*

Discuss the following:

- Describe an occasion when you were in a group and the talk turned ugly about someone who was not there. What happened? What did you learn from the situation?
- Most people know of a time when they were the one being talked about at a gathering they didn't attend. How did you feel when it happened to you?
- What harm would it do for Susan to remain silent?

In the last chapter you learned to identify the tempter. This chapter will show you how to identify one of his most popular techniques—LET'S MAKE A DEAL!

WHAT'S OUR EXAMPLE?

Take turns reading Luke 4:1–13 again.

¹Jesus, full of the Holy Spirit, returned from the Jordan and was led by the Spirit in the desert, ²where for forty days he was tempted by the devil. He ate nothing during those days, and at the end of them he was hungry.

³The devil said to him, "If you are the Son of God, tell this stone to become bread."

⁴Jesus answered, "It is written: 'Man does not live on bread alone.'"

⁵The devil led him up to a high place and showed him in an instant all the kingdoms of the world. ⁶And he said to him, "I will give you all their authority and splendor, for it has been given to me, and I can give it to anyone I want to. ⁷So if you worship me, it will all be yours."

⁸Jesus answered, "It is written: 'Worship the Lord your God and serve him only.'"

⁹The devil led him to Jerusalem and had him stand on the highest point of the temple. "If you are the Son of God," he said, "throw yourself down from here. ¹⁰For it is written:

'He will command his angels
concerning you
to guard you carefully;
¹¹they will lift you up in their hands,
so that you will not strike your
foot against a stone.'"

¹²Jesus answered, "It says: 'Do not put the Lord your God to the test.'"

¹³When the devil had finished all this tempting, he left him until an opportune time.

WHAT'S THE ANSWER?

The first time the devil tempted Jesus, Jesus recognized him and turned down his enticing suggestion. But Satan didn't give up after one try. He came back to Jesus with an offer Satan thought was too good to refuse! "Have I got a deal for you!" he urged.

When the devil first tempted Jesus to make a loaf of bread to ease His intense hunger, Jesus recognized the temptation and reminded the devil of God's Word. Verse 4 is a quotation from Deuteronomy 8:3, which records a time when God's people were hungry and God promised to take care of them. Bread is important to satisfy physical hunger, but true satisfaction comes from the Word of God. Jesus' trust was not in His own ability to create bread, but in His Father who is the bread of life.

When the devil tempts us to take the easy way out, we can use God's Word to tell him to get lost. God has promised to satisfy us, so we don't need Satan's shortcuts. Tell yourself, "If I need to cheat to have this, then I don't need it. God has something better for me."

Since Satan is a spirit and has spiritual powers, he was able to show Jesus the kingdoms of the world in a spectacular way! Imagine looking out of an airplane window at the civilization below you. Perhaps this was the kind of scene Satan held up before Jesus. Then he said, "I will give you all of this if you will worship me!" The devil was offering immediate power

and importance. "No need to suffer and die to gain it, Jesus. I can give it to you NOW," Satan tempted.

Let's make a deal! Worship me, and I'll give you everything you see!

If Jesus had given in, what would He have gotten? The world Satan offered had already been ruined by sin. God had sent Jesus to conquer sin, not to rule over a sinful world. Throughout history the devil has found many leaders who snatched up this offer, only to find that their empire is full of sin and death. To win over evil, Jesus had to take the worst punishment a sinful world could give without giving in to sin Himself. If He would do that, God promised Him heaven, a world with no sin at all.

In the long run, whose deal was better? Satan's or God's? Why?

Jesus answered with God's Word again. Verse 8 is quoted from Deuteronomy 6:13.

When the devil tempts you to make anything more important than God, he is asking you to trade eternal benefits for temporary pleasure. You already have everything as an heir of God through Jesus. What more could there be? Don't be fooled by the devil's deals. Tell him no!

BACK TO SQUARE ONE

Give some thought to Susan's situation.

• What harm would be done if she joined in the gossip?
• Can you identify for her exactly what trade the devil is tempting her to make?
• If she makes this trade, what problems do you foresee?

This might seem like a harmless sin, but it may not seem so harmless the next time she finds herself in this situation. One little sin leads to another. Try to explain to Susan how this could snowball into a bigger problem.

Advice is easier to give than to follow. Next time you are caught in a similar situation, what will you do? Discuss some possible ways out of a tricky situation like this. Remember that making a deal with the devil (even a little tiny one) is letting him control you.

MOVING AHEAD

Some things seem so important to us that we lose all perspective in acquiring them. Job status, grades, popularity, acceptance, and comfort can all motivate us to make compromises.

Let's find out how to spot the devil's "Let's Make A Deal" tactics and analyze what he's really offering and what it will cost.

- Write on a piece of paper some of the deals you can think of. (If you will just . . . I will make you . . . .)
- Will the things promised last?
- Will what you gain benefit anyone other than yourself?
- Is it worth what you have to give up?
- Can you take it to the Lord in a prayer of thanks?
- The next time Satan offers you a deal, ask yourself "What would Jesus do?"
- Keep a record of your thoughts and experiences on the "Keeping Track" page.

Whatever the devil promises has been ruined by sin. Don't make any foolish trades. Talk over issues like this when they seem confusing. Always consider them alongside God's Word.

QUOTES & STUFF

Character is much easier kept than recovered. —*Thomas Paine*

Most men, when they think they are thinking, are merely rearranging their prejudices. —*Knute Rockne*

The Great Wall of China is a gigantic structure that cost an immense amount of money and labor. When it was finished it appeared impregnable. But three times the enemy breached it— not by breaking it down or going around it. They did it by bribing the gatekeepers.

JUST FOR FUN

- New York has a law forbidding blind men from driving automobiles.

- In Rutland, Vermont, it is illegal to let your car backfire.

- In Milwaukee an ordinance says that no automobile can be parked over two hours unless hitched to a horse.

- In Memphis it is against the law for a woman to drive a car unless there is a man either running or walking in front of the car waving a red flag to warn approaching motorists and pedestrians.

KEEPING TRACK

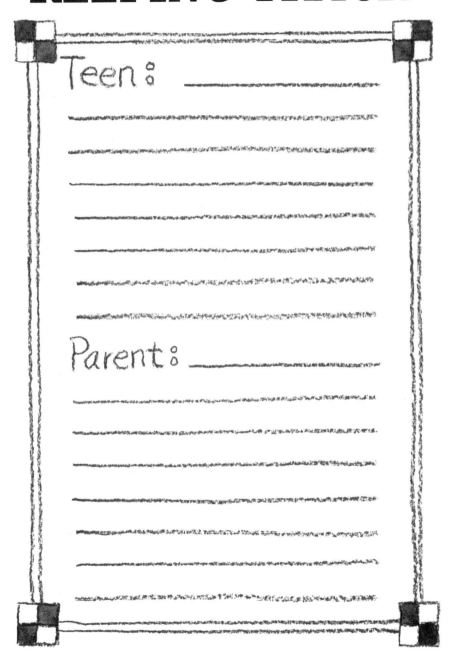

Teen: _____

_____

_____

_____

_____

_____

_____

Parent: _____

_____

_____

_____

_____

_____

_____

FIVE

I Can't Believe My Luck!

Do not put the Lord your God to the test.

LUKE 4:12

Brian and his older brother, Tom, spent the better part of Thursday night going over the things that would be on Brian's math exam. Although Brian was a good student, math was not his best subject and the final exam had him a little worried. Friday morning at breakfast the boys went over the formulas one more time and Brian was pleased at how much he could remember. Tom was pleased too and told Brian so. It meant a lot to Brian to have the admiration of his big brother. The boys reviewed questions all the way to school and then parted with a thumbs up sign for good luck. Brian's exam was the last class of the day and when it finally arrived, he felt ready.

Brian walked into the classroom and over to his seat. He noticed some pencil marks around the edges of his desk but didn't pay much attention to them because the test was being handed out and instructions given. "Just do your best," he heard the teacher say.

Brian worked hard on the first problem and was pleased with how easily he solved it. He was even more pleased when his answer appeared as one of the choices at the end of the question. As he darkened the appropriate circle on the answer sheet he noticed again the writing on his desk. There was a

number 1 with something scratched next to it. It was the answer! He quickly worked the second problem and found that it too corresponded with the answer next to the number 2 on the desk. His face grew red and hot as he realized that someone in the class before him had written all of the answers to this test on his desk top!

Discuss the following:

- Describe a time when you were in a situation like Brian's.
- On a scale of 1 to 5, how would you rate the way you handled it?
- Brian has stumbled into a compromising situation. What options does he have?
- What things does he need to consider when deciding what to do?
- Brian is a Christian. What difference should that make in his decision?

Brian is being tempted to make himself look good by doing something that doesn't honor God. Jesus faced a temptation like this. Satan's solution to Jesus' dilemma appeared to be a harmless and easy way out of a hard situation. When you see how Jesus handled it, you may be able to give Brian some wise advice.

Remember who the tempter is. He has nothing to gain by tempting you to do something that has no consequences.

WHAT'S OUR EXAMPLE?

Take turns reading Luke 4:1–13 again.

¹Jesus, full of the Holy Spirit, returned from the Jordan and was led by the Spirit in the desert, ²where for forty days he was tempted by the devil. He ate nothing during those days, and at the end of them he was hungry.

³The devil said to him, "If you are the Son of God, tell this stone to become bread."

⁴Jesus answered, "It is written: 'Man does not live on bread alone.'"

⁵The devil led him up to a high place and showed him in an instant all the kingdoms of the world. ⁶And he said to him, "I will give you all their authority and splendor, for it has been given to me, and I can give it to anyone I want to. ⁷So if you worship me, it will all be yours."

⁸Jesus answered, "It is written: 'Worship the Lord your God and serve him only.'"

⁹The devil led him to Jerusalem and had him stand on the highest point of the temple. "If you are the Son of God," he said, "throw yourself down from here. ¹⁰For it is written:

'He will command his angels
concerning you
to guard you carefully;
¹¹they will lift you up in their hands,
so that you will not strike your
foot against a stone.'"

¹²Jesus answered, "It says: 'Do not put the Lord your God to the test.'"

¹³When the devil had finished all this tempting, he left him until an opportune time.

WHAT'S THE ANSWER?

Somehow, we're not exactly sure how, Jesus and Satan wound up at the top of the temple, a huge building with high walls. In the courtyards below were the people Jesus loved, the important religious men whom Jesus wanted to convince that He was God's son, and the chosen people of Israel whom Jesus came to save.

Satan knew how important this mission was to Jesus, so he suggested a shortcut Jesus could take to convince the people He was their Messiah. It sounded reasonable. And the results Satan promised were certainly good.

"Just throw yourself down from here in front of them all, and they will have to believe you!" the devil prodded. To make it sound even better, he quoted Scripture to Jesus! What a diabolical enemy!

Have you ever heard someone who doesn't love God use His Word as an excuse for doing something wrong? Have you ever heard someone shout "an eye for an eye" while executing a vengeful punch in the face? How about "eat, drink and be merry, for tomorrow we die" as an excuse for selfish indulgence. God's Word never gives an excuse to be selfish or to dishonor God.

Jesus saw through this trick. He understood that the

devil was daring him to prove God's Word by showing off, and Jesus answered him by using God's Word properly. Look at verse 12 (also see Deuteronomy 6:16). God's Word never needs to be tested. The promises in God's Word are for people who honor and obey Him, not to prove a point or show off.

If Jesus had given in to this temptation and thrown Himself off the temple, how would that have affected God's plan of salvation?

The temptation to show off is a hard one to ignore. After all, who doesn't like to look good in front of others? The problem with showing off is that it may bring short term glory to you, but it dishonors God. Jesus would not dishonor His Father, and if we obey His example neither will we.

Jesus defeated the devil. Verse 13 says that the devil left Him until a later time. We can defeat the devil when temptations come our way. Jesus beat him with the Word of God, and so can we. Read 1 Corinthians 10:13. This is a promise. When temptation comes, there will always be a way of escape. God always allows us to choose to defeat the devil. As life goes on, temptations just get bigger. Learn to spot the way of escape God provides in every tempting situation.

BACK TO SQUARE ONE

Give some thought to Brian's situation.

- If you could put three thoughts into Brian's head, what would they be?
- What might be some of the consequences of using the answers on his desk?
- Adults face this temptation frequently. Opportunities often come up to take the credit for someone else's work. How should adults respond when the only way for them to look good is to pretend someone else's accomplishment is their own?

This is war. The worst thing Brian or anyone else can do is to convince themselves that some sins are little and don't really matter. That is what the devil wants you to think. Your best chance of winning is to recognize the enemy, remember that God will always provide an escape for you, and make sure you choose to do what honors God. If John 14:23 is true, and God comes to live in you, you have the power to win every battle against Satan.

What do you think Jesus would advise Brian to do? What do you think you would do?

MOVING AHEAD

Just as you locate the emergency exits in an airplane or a crowded theater, you need to be able to identify the escape routes God places in every tight spot you face. Whenever a situation arises that tempts you to cheat, to take credit you don't deserve, or to praise yourself above God, the exits will be clearly marked.

• Watch for situations in your life this week that tempt you to dishonor God.
• Try to identify your options and determine a way of escape.
• Make a few notes about what you learn so you can talk about them the next time you meet together.
• Consider becoming a way of escape for each other. A phone call might be just the thing to help you out of one of those situations.
• Keep a record of your thoughts and experiences on the "Keeping Track" page.

QUOTES & STUFF

If a man does not keep pace with his companions, perhaps it is because he hears a different drummer. Let him step to the music which he hears, however measured or far away. —*Henry David Thoreau*

Better keep yourself clean and bright; you are the window through which you must see the world. —*George Bernard Shaw*

JUST FOR FUN

Animal Trivia. Did you know . . .

- The Tokyo Zoo in Japan is closed for two months a year to give the animals a vacation from the people.

- Jellyfish sometimes evaporate.

- Pigs can run a 7½-minute mile.

- Fish can become seasick if kept on board ship.

- Armadillos can be housebroken.

- In many species of birds the eyes weigh more than the brain.

- It takes four hours to hardboil the thirty-pound ostrich egg.

KEEPING TRACK

Teen: _____

_____

_____

_____

_____

_____

Parent: _____

_____

_____

_____

_____

_____

SIX

Why? Uh, because . . .

Then a cloud appeared and enveloped them, and a voice came from the cloud: "This is my Son, whom I love. Listen to him!"

MARK 9:7

Cindy had grown up in a Christian home. She had always gone to church and Sunday school, to church camp in the summer, and most of her weekends were spent with her church youth group. She had given her heart to the Lord at the age of five.

One weekend the youth group went downtown to do some evangelism. They cleaned up a neighborhood park and set up a lemonade and cookie stand for the kids there. The youth leaders said that showing God's love in this way would bring opportunities to witness. Cindy didn't give the outing much thought. It was just another day to spend with her friends.

As Cindy poured a glass of lemonade for a young man about her age he asked her why she was there.

"This is my church youth group," she responded.

Apparently unsatisfied with her answer, he asked again why she was there.

"Because we want to help people," she answered.

"But why?" he asked.

"Because we are Christians!" Cinty blurted, hoping he would just go away.

The young man was genuinely interested in Christianity,

but each time Cindy tried to answer his question he pushed for a more meaningful answer. Cindy looked around for help, but all the counselors and kids were busy. She wanted to witness, but her answers seemed so inadequate! *I've been a Christian all my life,* she thought. *What can I say? What if he doesn't believe me? God will be so disappointed with the way I do this! I wish I just had some sort of proof that what I say is true!*

Discuss the following:

- Describe a time when you were in a situation like Cindy's.
- Have you ever tried to explain what you believe to someone else? If so, explain what it felt like the first time.
- What do you do when someone asks hard questions that you don't have a ready answer for?
- Explain what you believe in three sentences.
- What proof do you have to back that up?

This is a difficult lesson. What God has done for us is such a complex thing, and yet we need to be able to explain it in simple terms. We need to know where to find proof that what we believe is true. Is it wrong to ask for proof?

Jesus urged people to check out the evidence. The Old Testament is historical evidence that supports New Testament claims. Jesus also took the time to give direct evidence to those first believers. The proof is there. Let's look at a time when Jesus gave His friends the proof they needed to see.

WHAT'S OUR EXAMPLE?

Take turns reading Mark 9:2–13.

²After six days Jesus took Peter, James and John with him and led them up a high mountain, where they were all alone. There he was transfigured before them. ³His clothes became dazzling white, whiter than anyone in the world could bleach them. ⁴And there appeared before them Elijah and Moses, who were talking with Jesus.

⁵Peter said to Jesus, "Rabbi, it is good for us to be here. Let us put up three shelters—one for you, one for Moses and one for Elijah." ⁶(He did not know what to say, they were so frightened.)

⁷Then a cloud appeared and enveloped them, and a voice came from the cloud: "This is my Son, whom I love. Listen to him!"

⁸Suddenly, when they looked around, they no longer saw anyone with them except Jesus.

⁹As they were coming down the mountain, Jesus gave them orders not to tell anyone what they had seen until the Son of Man had risen from the dead. ¹⁰They kept the matter to themselves, discussing what "rising from the dead" meant.

¹¹And they asked him, "Why do the teachers of the law say that Elijah must come first?"

¹²Jesus replied, "To be sure, Elijah does come first, and restores all things. Why then is it written that the Son of Man must suffer much and be rejected? ¹³But I tell you, Elijah has come, and they have done to him everything they wished, just as it is written about him."

W^{HAT'S}THE ANSWER?

Jesus took Peter, James, and John on a little side trip and left the other nine disciples to minister to the crowds. Jesus knew how hard it was for His disciples to learn the things He was teaching them. They had lived with Him as a friend, as a man. They walked and worked and got tired together. Even though they loved Him and they believed in what He said, those days before the resurrection of Jesus were confusing. If He was indeed the Son of God, why didn't things go more smoothly for Him? Why did the religious leaders give them such a hard time?

Why did Jesus single out these three men? Look up Mark 5:37 and Mark 14:33. Persecution was coming. Death and apparent defeat were coming. Jesus knew that these three friends would be the leaders in His church. Their faith must be solid, unshakable.

Try to explain what the situation in verse 3 might have been like. (Look up Matthew 17:2–3 and Luke 9:29–31.) To a Jew, the men spoken of in verse 4 were heros! Imagine the impact it would have on you to see Abraham Lincoln and Benjamin Franklin talking with your friend.

In verses 8–9 things got back to normal, sort of. Jesus asked them to keep this a secret for a while. Can you think of a reason why He wouldn't want all the disciples to know about this?

Jesus' death still didn't make any sense to these three. Especially after what they had seen. How could anyone think that this great man would really die? In verses 11–13, who was

Jesus talking about? (See Matthew 17:13.) This was a prophecy that had to be fulfilled before the Messiah could save the people. (See Malachi 4:5.) Jesus told them that, just as no one recognized John the Baptist as Elijah, no one would recognize Jesus as the Messiah. Jesus knew that the time He had left with His friends was getting short, and He wanted to give them proof that the things that were about to happen were in God's plan.

Jesus was teaching a lesson in love and confidence! The disciples loved Him. They were with Him every day and yet they had trouble understanding things. There were things they couldn't explain when others questioned their faith in Him.

Do you ever have times when you don't understand something about God? Are you ever unsure how to explain your faith to someone else? Jesus understood when His friends struggled with this, and He understands when we do too. For his friends He provided a glimpse of glory! For us He has provided the completed story of God's plan. The Old Testament history is accurate and verifiable. It makes predictions that were fulfilled in the New Testament. Historically speaking, there is just too much evidence to deny. Also He has given the Holy Spirit to those who believe in Him. He teaches us what we need to verify our faith and gives us even more proof if we need it by involving Himself in our lives.

BACK TO SQUARE ONE

Give some thought to Cindy's situation.

- Cindy is afraid of letting God down. She is afraid that her faith won't stand for anything if she can't describe it well enough. What do you think? Can you give her any words of encouragement?
- Do you have any advice for Cindy before she tries to witness again? Could you benefit from this advice?
- If Jesus could have taken Cindy aside for a few quick moments of instruction, what do you think He would have told her to say or to do?

MOVING AHEAD

- Look up the following verses and note how they fit together.
    - Isaiah 7:14 & Matthew 1:18
    - Hosea 11:1 & Matthew 2:15
    - Micah 5:2 & Matthew 2:1
    - Zechariah 9:9 & Matthew 21:1–5
    - Zechariah 11:12 & Matthew 26:14
    - Zechariah 11:13 & Matthew 27:5–10
- Read Psalm 22 (which was written at a time when crucifixion was not known to Israel), and compare it to John 19. (Jesus quoted Psalm 22:1 in Matthew 27:46.)
- Study enough to find the evidence you need so that you can speak with conviction about what you know to be true. The fact that you are convinced and trust Jesus to be your Savior is the only witness God will require of you.
- Keep a record of your thoughts and experiences on the "Keeping Track" page.

There will be times when someone asks more questions than you are prepared to answer, but God has given us proof that His Word is true. That proof is the Word itself. Never be afraid to go to or to send someone else to the Bible for answers. The answers are all in there. Jesus asks you to be a witness to what He has done for you personally. If you can testify with confidence that Jesus is real to you, the Holy Spirit will help others find the proof they need to believe.

QUOTES & STUFF

God loves every one of us as if there were but one of us to love. —*Augustine*

He is no fool who gives up what he cannot keep to gain that which he cannot lose. —*Jim Elliot*

Yet I am not ashamed, because I know whom I have believed, and am convinced that he is able to guard what I have entrusted to him for that day. —*2 Timothy 1:12*

Sitting in a church doesn't make you a Christian any more than sitting in a garage makes you a car.

JUST FOR FUN

Be careful who you listen to. A smooth talker can make a case for almost anything.

black = dark	ugly = offensive
dark = obscure	offensive = insulting
obscure = hidden	insulting = insolent
hidden = enveloped	insolent = proud
enveloped = snug	proud = lordly
snug = comfortable	lordly = stately
comfortable = easy	stately = grand
easy = simple	grand = gorgeous
simple = pure	gorgeous = beautiful
pure = white	Therefore ugly = beautiful
Therefore black = white	

KEEPING TRACK

Teen: _____

_____

_____

_____

_____

_____

_____

Parent: _____

_____

_____

_____

_____

_____

_____

SEVEN

It's Just Not Fair!

Jesus said, "Everything is possible for him who believes." Immediately the boy's father exclaimed, "I do believe; help me overcome my unbelief!"

MARK 9:23–24

Sam let the heavy gym door thud behind him before he let out the tremendous sigh of relief he'd been keeping inside. This was too good to be true! He really hadn't thought he would make the varsity soccer team, but there was his name on the roster! Dad would be so proud!

Sam ran the entire way home. When he reached his driveway he stopped to compose himself so he could walk in really cool. He wanted to just sort of let his good news slip out, but he couldn't seem to control the smile plastered across his face.

As soon as Sam walked through the door he knew something was wrong. His father and mother were seated at the dining room table and his mother's eyes were full of tears. Sam couldn't believe how quickly his world was crumbling as his father broke the news to him. Once again his dad's company was transfering him to a new city.

The news hit Sam like a blast of hot air. He didn't know what to say or do, so he just stood there silently for what seemed like a very long time. His mother's voice was the trigger that brought all of his emotions to the surface. "Are you okay, Sam?"

"Oh sure, I'm just fine! Let's not worry about good old Sam! Let's not even consider how he feels about having his life

ripped apart and thrown down the sewer!"

Sam ran up the stairs to his room and slammed the door so hard that two pictures fell off the wall. Through hot tears he saw his Bible still open from his morning devotions. "Where is God now?" he moaned as he knocked it to the floor. He flopped down on his bed. "It's just not fair."

Discuss the following:

Tell about a time when you faced bitter disappointment like Sam's.

• How did you feel?
• What action did you take?
• How did God fit into the situation?

Sometimes the answers we seek aren't found easily, and sometimes our circumstances aren't all we want them to be. The following Scripture gives some insight into how Jesus responds to our problems and it tells where we can go to find the answers we need.

WHAT'S OUR EXAMPLE?

Take turns reading Mark 9:14–29.

14When they came to the other disciples, they saw a large crowd around them and the teachers of the law arguing with them. 15As soon as all the people saw Jesus, they were overwhelmed with wonder and ran to greet him.

16"What are you arguing with them about?" he asked.

17A man in the crowd answered, "Teacher, I brought you my son, who is possessed by a spirit that has robbed him of speech. 18Whenever it seizes him, it throws him to the ground. He foams at the mouth, gnashes his teeth and becomes rigid. I asked your disciples to drive out the spirit, but they could not."

19"O unbelieving generation," Jesus replied, "how long shall I stay with you? How long shall I put up with you? Bring the boy to me."

20So they brought him. When the spirit saw Jesus, it immediately threw the boy into a convulsion. He fell to the ground and rolled around, foaming at the mouth.

21Jesus asked the boy's father, "How long has he been like this?"

"From childhood," he answered. ²²"It has often thrown him into fire or water to kill him. But if you can do anything, take pity on us and help us."

²³"'If you can'?" said Jesus. "Everything is possible for him who believes."

²⁴Immediately the boy's father exclaimed, "I do believe; help me overcome my unbelief!"

²⁵When Jesus saw that a crowd was running to the scene, he rebuked the evil spirit. "You deaf and mute spirit," he said, "I command you, come out of him and never enter him again."

²⁶The spirit shrieked, convulsed him violently and came out. The boy looked so much like a corpse that many said, "He's dead." ²⁷But Jesus took him by the hand and lifted him to his feet, and he stood up.

²⁸After Jesus had gone indoors, his disciples asked him privately, "Why couldn't we drive it out?"

²⁹He replied, "This kind can come out only by prayer."

W<u>HAT'S</u> THE ANSWER?

While Peter, James, and John were on the mountain with Jesus (our previous lesson), the other nine disciples were having a problem! Notice who is causing all the commotion (v. 14). The teachers of the law always seemed to be close by, trying to trick Jesus. What things might have been said in this argument?

Suppose you were one of those disciples. You had seen Jesus do miraculous things and had even experienced that power yourself. Suddenly you have the chance to do a big miracle in front of all the right people. But it won't work! What could be wrong? You try again, but no miracle. You stop for a minute and think. *Is there anything I forgot to do?*

Jesus was upset. He had done so many miracles for the people and all they wanted was to trick him. Why couldn't they recognize Him as God's Son? Which one recognized instantly who He was (v. 20)? Does that surprise you?

This father must have loved his child a lot. If the son had been this way from birth, the father must have been constantly watching out for his safety. How exhausting! Do you think the father believed Jesus could help his son or was he just hoping (v. 22)?

Jesus told the man to believe (v. 23), but believing is a hard thing to do sometimes. Notice what the father said to Jesus in verse 24. Many times people have trouble believing in some part or all of the Bible. Many times people have doubts. What are some of your doubts?

Jesus taught that having doubts is not a sin. Did Jesus get mad at the man for admitting that he had trouble believing? What did Jesus do to help the man believe?

When you have a doubt or question about your faith, don't keep it to yourself, and don't take it to another doubter. Take your question to Jesus and ask Him to help you with it. There is an answer in God's Word, so don't be afraid to ask. God gives special insights to some people, and they can help you find the answers you can't find for yourself. That is what pastors and older Christians are for. Ask the hard questions. Jesus doesn't mind doubts and questions if they are from someone seeking a truthful answer.

The disciples forgot to do something important when they were trying to solve the problem (v. 29). What was it? This is always the first step in successfully solving any problem.

BACK TO SQUARE ONE

Give some thought to Sam's problem.

- What can you do for him? Perhaps the first thing is to listen and be quiet. Jesus listened carefully to the man's whole story before doing anything. Why do you think Jesus did so when He already knew the situation?
- Who else might Sam tell his problem to?
- What would you tell Sam about obeying Jesus in a situation like this?
- Have you ever had to just trust and wait?
- What about Sam's mother? She was obviously upset by the news. What do you think her response to Sam should be?
- How might they help each other make something good out of this problem?
- Is it all right for Sam to be sad? Is it possible to be sad without giving in to despair?

Bad times come unexpectedly. To prepare for them we can arm ourselves with God's promises and power before we're in the middle of the battle.

MOVING AHEAD

It's easy to trust God when everything is going well, but when things take an unpleasant turn we sometimes forget who is in control. Despair is a new disguise for an old enemy, and when we give in to despair we let the devil control us. Identifying the enemy will help us overcome him and get back on track. (Remember, God can turn any situation into good. Satan wants to take that hope away and replace it with despair.)

- Identify one tough problem (yours or someone else's).
- Ask God to help you find His good answer for this problem.
- Write out five good things that could come out of this situation.
- Discuss your problems and help each other find something good in the situation.
- Keep a record of your thoughts and experiences on the "Keeping Track" page.

Perhaps the hardest step to take is to move from wanting to feel bad about the situation to wanting to see good in it. That takes supernatural power. That power is available to you.

QUOTES & STUFF

You are limited only to those things to which you limit yourself. —*Mike Singletary.*

If all our misfortunes were laid in one common heap, whence everyone must take an equal portion, most people would be contented to take their own and depart. —*Socrates*

JUST FOR FUN

This puzzle should keep you busy for a while. Answers can be found on the "Quotes and Stuff" page of the next chapter.

What is . . .

1. 7 W of the A W
2. 1001 A N
3. 9 P in the SS
4. 88 K on a P
5. 13 S on the A F
6. 32 D F at which W F
7. 18 H on a G C
8. 90 D in a R A
9. 8 S on a S S
10. 3 B M (SHTR)
11. 4 Q in a G
12. 24 H in a D
13. 1 W on a U
14. 5 D in a Z C
15. 11 P on a F T
16. 29 D in F in a L Y
17. 64 S on a C
18. 40 D and N of the G F

(This appeared in the Raleigh News and Observer*)*

KEEPING TRACK

Teen: _____

_____
_____
_____
_____
_____
_____

Parent: _____

_____
_____
_____
_____
_____
_____

EIGHT

Let's Put First Things First

Mary . . . sat at the Lord's feet listening
to what he said

LUKE 10:39

Mary Baxter is a wonderful teacher. Her students love her because she brings such excitement to the classroom. She makes learning fun by encouraging students to work on special projects. A lot of people are saying that this is the year she will be named Teacher of the Year. This semester she is working with two student teachers from the state university and is finishing up her master's degree in the evenings. She's almost always the first one at school in the mornings and the last to leave in the afternoons.

The Baxter children are in high school and their schedules are full of lessons and sports. Mary manages to get everybody to the right place at the right time. She sings in the choir at church, teaches a Sunday school class, and has just been elected president of the Women's Guild. She keeps her home clean enough for company and entertains as often as she can. Sometimes her daughter, Melissa, feels like she needs an appointment just to see her mom.

One Saturday afternoon Melissa came in the back door and found her mother crying as she put clothes into the washing machine. Melissa's heart raced as she put her hand on her mother's shoulder.

"Mom, what's wrong?"

"Oh, nothing," her mother replied. After a few quiet moments she turned to face her daughter. "It's just that I feel like such a failure! There is so much to do and I don't feel like I do anything really well. I'm just so tired."

Melissa was stunned. How could Mrs. Wonderful feel like a failure?

Discuss the following:

- Describe a time when you felt like a failure. What made you feel that way?
- Have you ever "bitten off more than you could chew"?
- Do you know any overachievers?
- What do you think drives people to push themselves so hard?
- Why do you think Mrs. Baxter feels like a failure?
- Does it strike you as odd that someone who does so much would feel so bad about herself?
- How would you expect Melissa to react to her mom's confession?
- If you were Mrs. Baxter, what would you really like Melissa to say to you?

Jesus had a friend in similar turmoil. He may not have said the words she wanted to hear, but He gave her some advice she desperately needed. After this chapter you should be able to help Mary Baxter put her problem into perspective.

WHAT'S OUR EXAMPLE?

Take turns reading Luke 10:38–42.

³⁸As Jesus and his disciples were on their way, he came to a village where a woman named Martha opened her home to him. ³⁹She had a sister called Mary, who sat at the Lord's feet listening to what he said. ⁴⁰But Martha was distracted by all the preparations that had to be made. She came to him and asked, "Lord, don't you care that my sister has left me to do the work by myself? Tell her to help me!"

⁴¹"Martha, Martha," the Lord answered, "you are worried and upset about many things, ⁴²but only one thing is needed. Mary has chosen what is better, and it will not be taken away from her."

Also read John 12:1–3.

¹Six days before the Passover, Jesus arrived at Bethany, where Lazarus lived, whom Jesus had raised from the dead. ²Here a dinner was given in Jesus' honor. Martha served, while Lazarus was among those reclining at the table with him. ³Then Mary took about a pint of pure nard, an expensive perfume; she poured it on Jesus' feet and wiped his feet with her hair. And the house was filled with the fragrance of the perfume.

W^{HAT'S} THE ANSWER?

Mary, Martha, and Lazarus (their brother) were good friends of Jesus. Their home in Bethany, which was about two miles from Jersualem, was the place where Jesus often rested after much walking and teaching.

What preparations do you think Martha was making (v. 40)? Jesus was not coming alone, so there were a lot of things she thought needed to be done. Think of a time when important company came to your home to visit. What things had to be done?

If you were the one rushing around doing all of the chores and Mary was your sister, how would you feel? Try to put Martha's complaint into your own words.

This is a frustrating situation! There is too much work and not enough time. When you are doing your best, going your fastest, and still there is more to do, it is easy to lash out at the people around you whom you think should be helping.

See what Jesus said (vv. 41–42). What was Mary doing that was more important than fixing supper for Jesus (v. 39)? What do you think He was talking about that had Mary so interested? Imagine having Jesus right there with you and being able to listen to His voice and ask Him questions.

Jesus said that only one thing was needed (v. 42). King David, from the Old Testament, found that one thing (Psalm 27:4). What was it?

Jesus wasn't teaching that it was all right to be lazy. He

wasn't teaching that we should let others do all the work or that work isn't important. He was teaching that nothing is as important as seeking God. When we let other things become our focus, we forget to listen to His voice and ask Him questions. Entertainment, sports, and hobbies can take up all of our free time. Working hard to make money or a good name can become all-consuming. Even committee meetings, good deeds, and obligations can take up time that we should spend seeking that one thing.

Jesus was giving a clear example of how to keep everything in our lives in the proper priority. To please Jesus we need to keep things in perspective. If we spend time at Jesus' feet before doing anything else, we will see everything we have to do from His perspective instead of ours.

BACK TO SQUARE ONE

Give some thought to Mrs. Baxter's problem.

• What makes her so busy? If all the things she does are so important, why does she feel so bad about doing them? What will happen if she doesn't do some of those things?
• After reading this chapter, what encouragement or advice would you give Mrs. Baxter?
• If Jesus were to sit down with Mrs. Baxter, what would He suggest?

MOVING AHEAD

Many overworked people are trying to prove to others or to themselves that they are important. Sitting at the feet of Jesus will show a person that they are already important and will take some of the load off their shoulders. Starting the day in God's Word and in prayer won't make a busy schedule easier, but it will help us make wise choices about what is really important. Look at your schedule in light of the story you've just read.

- Which sister are you most like? Mary or Martha?
- Write down three things a Christian can do every day to obey Jesus and find that one important thing?
- Think about your average day. Write down the five things that you spend most of your time doing while you are awake.
- Are any of the things from your first list on your second list?
- For the next five days, get up early enough to spend ten minutes reading your Bible and five minutes praying. Ask God to help you make Him the most important thing in your life.
- Keep a record of your thoughts and experiences on the "Keeping Track" page.

QUOTES & STUFF

I have so much to do today that I shall spend the first three hours in prayer. —*Martin Luther*

If Christians do not "come apart and rest a while," they may just plain come apart! —*Vance Havner*

J. S. Bach signed all of his work SDG, which means *Soli Deo Gloria*, only to God be the glory.

JUST FOR FUN

In the 1880s the help wanted ads included the following: "Wanted: young, skinny, wiry fellows not over 18. Must be expert riders, willing to risk death daily. Orphans preferred. Wages $25.00 a week." —*The Pony Express*

Answers to last month's puzzle:

1. 7 wonders of the ancient world.
2. 1001 Arabian Nights.
3. 9 planets in the solar system.
4. 88 keys on a piano
5. 13 stripes on an American flag.
6. 32 degrees Fahrenheit at which water freezes.
7. 18 holes on a golf course
8. 90 degrees in a right angle
9. 8 sides on a stop sign
10. 3 blind mice (see how they run).
11. 4 quarts in a gallon (or 4 quarters in a game).
12. 24 hours in a day.
13. 1 wheel on a unicycle.
14. 5 digits in a zip code.
15. 11 players on a football team.
16. 29 days in February in a leap year.
17. 64 squares on a checkerboard.
18. 40 days and nights of the great flood.

KEEPING TRACK

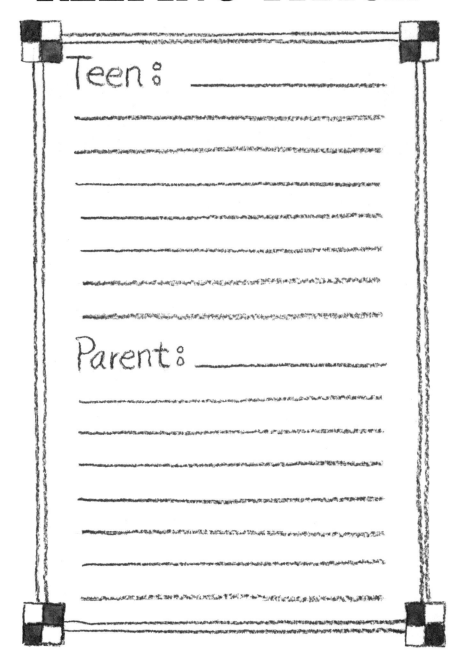

Teen: _____

Parent: _____

NINE

Excuse Me, God, But There Seems to Be Some Mistake

"Lazarus is dead, and for your sake I am glad I was not there, so that you may believe."

JOHN 11:14

When Scott heard that his boss was going to hire an assistant he set his mind on getting the job. It would be perfect for him! The hours would be a little longer but the pay would be better, and the title certainly would impress people.

For weeks Scott did his best to act like an assistant manager in the pizza shop. He came in early a few times and made sure the extra little things in the kitchen were taken care of. He was the model employee. He even used his own time to train the owner's nephew. There was no doubt in Scott's mind that he would be getting the promotion.

Finally the day of the announcement came and Scott could hardly contain his excitement. He watched as the manager posted the yellow piece of paper on the bulletin board.

"Congratulations to David, our new Assistant Manager!"

What? David hadn't been there as long as Scott. He never did anything extra. Scott had never considered him a threat.

When quitting time came, Scott bolted out the door and raced to his car. He slammed the door, revved the engine, and screeched out of the parking lot. He was angry at the store

manager and even angrier at God. "This opportunity would have been perfect for me, God! Why did you let this happen?"

Discuss the following:

- Describe a time when you experienced disappointment like Scott's.
- What do you think about Scott's reaction to the news?
- If this was your problem, to whom could you go for help?
- How do you think a Christian should react to disappointment?

Jesus was surrounded by people who thought they knew what He needed to do to be Messiah. In the following story, Jesus teaches those closest to Him the importance of accepting God's plan and God's timing.

WHAT'S OUR EXAMPLE?

Take turns reading John 11:1–19.

¹Now a man named Lazarus was sick. He was from Bethany, the village of Mary and her sister Martha. ²This Mary, whose brother Lazarus now lay sick, was the same one who poured perfume on the Lord and wiped his feet with her hair. ³So the sisters sent word to Jesus, "Lord, the one you love is sick."

⁴When he heard this, Jesus said, "This sickness will not end in death. No, it is for God's glory so that God's Son may be glorified through it." ⁵Jesus loved Martha and her sister and Lazarus. ⁶Yet when he heard that Lazarus was sick, he stayed where he was two more days.

⁷Then he said to his disciples, "Let us go back to Judea." ⁸"But Rabbi," they said, "a short while ago the Jews tried to stone you, and yet you are going back there?"

⁹Jesus answered, "Are there not twelve hours of daylight? A man who walks by day will not stumble, for he sees by this world's light. ¹⁰It is when he walks by night that he stumbles, for he has no light."

¹¹After he had said this, he went on to tell them, "Our friend Lazarus has fallen asleep; but I am going there to wake him up."

¹²His disciples replied, "Lord, if he sleeps, he will get better." ¹³Jesus had been speaking of his death, but his disciples thought he meant natural sleep.

¹⁴So then he told them plainly, "Lazarus is dead, ¹⁵and for your sake I am glad I was not there, so that you may believe. But let us go to him."

¹⁶Then Thomas (called Didymus) said to the rest of the disciples, "Let us also go, that we may die with him."

¹⁷On his arrival, Jesus found that Lazarus had already been in the tomb for four days. ¹⁸Bethany was less than two miles from Jerusalem, ¹⁹and many Jews had come to Martha and Mary to comfort them in the loss of their brother.

WHAT'S THE ANSWER?

A little bit before Jesus received the news about Lazarus, He had healed a blind man on the Sabbath in the temple in Jerusalem. The teachers of the law wanted to stone Him for breaking the Sabbath. And not only that; Jesus also had called God His Father, which the religious leaders considered blasphemy.

The disciples were probably a bit on edge about being hated so much by such powerful people, so they wanted to stay as far away from Jerusalem as possible.

Then Jesus received a message from His friends Mary and Martha saying that their brother, Lazarus, was very sick. What do you think Mary and Martha expected Jesus to do when He heard the news? Jesus decided not to return right away, however (vv. 5–6). Why? What must the delay have been like for the sisters? Bethany was only two miles from Jerusalem, so what do you think the disciples were feeling at this time (vv. 7–8).

What was Jesus talking about in verses 9–10? Keep in mind that walking in darkness was very dangerous because there were no street lights and the roads were not paved. Was Jesus talking about walking at night or did He have another meaning in mind? Read John 9:4–5 and see if you can understand more clearly what Jesus meant. Perhaps He was reassuring the disciples that no one could harm Him until God's appointed time—until His work was done.

Thomas didn't totally understand what Jesus was saying, but still he was ready to follow Jesus (v. 16).

Add up the days recorded in this passage since Mary and Martha first sent the message. (Don't forget to include the messenger's traveling time. It was a full day's trip to Bethany.) Now read verse 17. Was Lazarus alive when Jesus got the message?

There was a superstition in those days that a person's spirit stayed close to the dead body for three days after death. During that time it could decide to return to the body. After that, all hope of life was gone. With this in mind, what reason do you think Jesus had for delaying His visit until four days had passed? Consider also that enough time had gone by for word to reach the Jews in Jerusalem who wanted to come and pay respects.

The disciples and the grieving sisters couldn't figure out what Jesus was doing. Lazarus needed Jesus, and Jesus seemed to have taken too much time getting there.

God was teaching a beautiful lesson about waiting for His timing. No matter how huge and urgent our problems may seem, ultimately they are in God's control. If we are going to trust Him to be Lord of our lives, we need to learn to trust Him to control the timing of every situation we face. We must learn to be patient, keep praying, and wait.

BACK TO SQUARE ONE

Give some thought to Scott's problem.

- If Scott was a member of your family, what could you say or do to comfort him? What would Jesus do first? Never try to give advice about a problem until you have taken the time to listen carefully to the one who is hurting. Sometimes advice isn't what is needed.
- List ways to comfort Scott without adding to his fury or belittling his problem.
- What temptations do you think the tempter might put before Scott? If you were Scott, what could you do in obedience to Jesus that would help you in this situation? Understanding why isn't the most important thing here. Trusting that God understands why is.

When we keep our eyes on Christ, obstacles become opportunities.

When the world around you is crumbling, God is the rock on which you can stand.

MOVING AHEAD

- Finish these sentences as you think the people in the text might have. It was difficult for these people to let go of their own idea of how things should be done.

    MARY: *Jesus, I wish you would . . .*

    MARTHA: *Jesus, I wish you would . .*

    THOMAS: *Jesus, I wish you would . . .*

- Think of a difficult situation in your life that you would like to have changed. Express your feelings by completing the following sentence.

    ME: *God, I wish you would . . .*

- Now that you have told Him how you would handle things, realize that He is in control and ask Him to show you how He intends to handle that situation. God's timing is perfect, even if it's not easy to understand. Can you trust Him enough to believe that?
- Keep a record of your thoughts and experiences on the "Keeping Track" page.

QUOTES & STUFF

"I asked God for strength that I might achieve.

I was made weak that I might learn humbly to obey.

I asked God for health that I might do greater things.

I was given infirmity that I might do better things.

I asked God for riches that I might be happy.

I was given poverty that I might be wise.

I asked God for power that I might have the praise of men.

I was given weakness that I might feel the need for God.

I asked for all things that I might enjoy life.

I was given life that I might enjoy all things.

I got nothing that I asked for, but everything I hoped for.

Almost despite myself, my unspoken prayers were answered.

I am among all men most richly blessed."

—*Unknown Confederate Soldier*

JUST FOR FUN

In 1832, Edwin Budding advertised his new invention like this: "Country gentlemen will find in using my machine an amusing, useful, and healthful exercise." Actually most of the healthful exercise went to the servants. Some teenagers today think the practice hasn't changed much. The invention? The lawnmower.

KEEPING TRACK

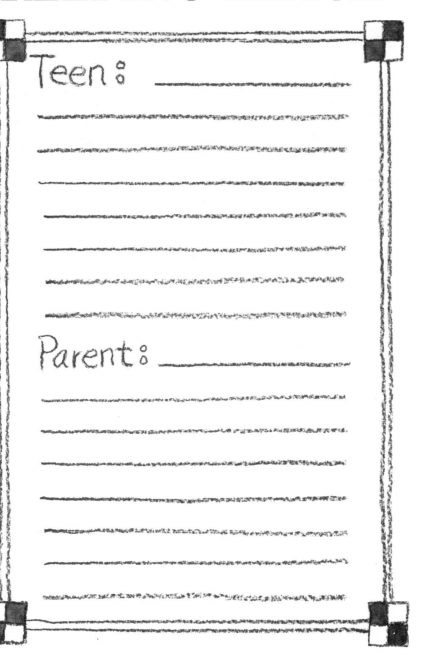

Teen: _____

_____

_____

_____

_____

_____

_____

Parent: _____

_____

_____

_____

_____

_____

_____

TEN

It's Hard to Let It Go

Then Jesus said, "Did I not tell you that
if you believed, you would see the glory
of God?"

JOHN 11:40

Everyone loves Holly—and has since she was a little girl. As a toddler she would go through the crowd after church and give hugs and kisses to all of the grownups. As she grew into a young woman, the whole church followed her accomplishments with pride. She was a good student and very popular with kids at school and at church. She often sang solos in church and took part in every play or pageant. She was a natural leader and no one was surprised when the youth group elected her president in her sophomore year. Hardly a week went by that she wasn't out several evenings for one reason or another.

When she went away to camp for the whole summer last year, everyone missed her. Holly didn't tell anyone that the camp she went to was a substance-abuse clinic.

At first she had been able to keep her drinking a secret from everyone. But when her grades began to slip and her temper began to flare more and more frequently, her parents confronted her. They were very supportive when they learned about her problem; Holly couldn't have asked for better help.

The summer away helped Holly put her life back together, and when school started again everything seemed to be all right.

But then one day you saw Holly all alone in the hallway with her head against her locker. When you asked her what was wrong she started to cry. She confided that she was struggling with two enemies in her life: her desire to drink and her guilt for having put her family through this whole thing. She said the second thing was by far the worse enemy.

Discuss the following:

- Describe a situation when you couldn't get rid of feelings of guilt.
- What did you do to deal with it?
- Did someone help you with the problem? What did the person say or do that helped?

In the last chapter we learned to trust God to take charge of our circumstances. This chapter will show us why. In Jesus Christ, there is power. Nice words and friendly encouragement will not be enough for Holly to overcome her problems. What she needs is power!

WHAT'S OUR EXAMPLE?

Take turns reading John 11:20–44.

²⁰When Martha heard that Jesus was coming, she went out to meet him, but Mary stayed at home.

²¹"Lord," Martha said to Jesus, "if you had been here, my brother would not have died. ²²But I know that even now God will give you whatever you ask."

²³Jesus said to her, "Your brother will rise again."

²⁴Martha answered, "I know he will rise again in the resurrection at the last day."

²⁵Jesus said to her, "I am the resurrection and the life. He who believes in me will live, even though he dies; ²⁶and whoever lives and believes in me will never die. Do you believe this?"

²⁷"Yes, Lord," she told him, "I believe that you are the Christ, the Son of God, who was to come into the world."

²⁸And after she had said this, she went back and called her sister Mary aside. "The Teacher is here," she said, "and is asking for you." ²⁹When Mary heard this, she got up quickly and went to him. ³⁰Now Jesus had not yet entered the village, but was still at the place where Martha had met him. ³¹When the Jews who had been with Mary in the house, comforting her, noticed how quickly she got up and went out, they followed her, supposing she was going to the tomb to mourn there.

³²When Mary reached the place where Jesus was and saw him, she fell at his feet and said, "Lord, if you had been here, my brother

would not have died."

³³When Jesus saw her weeping, and the Jews who had come along with her also weeping, he was deeply moved in spirit and troubled. ³⁴"Where have you laid him?" he asked.

"Come and see, Lord," they replied.

³⁵Jesus wept.

³⁶Then the Jews said, "See how he loved him!"

³⁷But some of them said, "Could not he who opened the eyes of the blind man have kept this man from dying?"

³⁸Jesus, once more deeply moved, came to the tomb. It was a cave with a stone laid across the entrance. ³⁹"Take away the stone," he said.

"But, Lord," said Martha, the sister of the dead man, "by this time there is a bad odor, for he has been there four days."

⁴⁰Then Jesus said, "Did I not tell you that if you believed, you would see the glory of God?"

⁴¹So they took away the stone. Then Jesus looked up and said, "Father, I thank you that you have heard me. ⁴²I knew that you always hear me, but I said this for the benefit of the people standing here, that they may believe that you sent me."

⁴³When he had said this, Jesus called in a loud voice, "Lazarus, come out!" ⁴⁴The dead man came out, his hands and feet wrapped with strips of linen, and a cloth around his face.

Jesus said to them, "Take off the grave clothes and let him go."

WHAT'S THE ANSWER?

When Martha heard that Jesus was coming she ran to meet Him. Do you detect any frustration in her comment (v. 21)? Any hope (v. 22)? Jesus told her that her brother would rise again, but Martha had trouble believing Him.

Have you ever been in the stands at a close basketball game and seen people covering their eyes—taking only a little peek now and then because they were afraid to hope? Perhaps that was Martha's dilemma. She was afraid to hope.

When Martha stated her belief in the resurrection that will come someday, Jesus said, "I **am** the resurrection!" Notice He didn't say I **will be** the resurrection. What does this mean to you? What did it mean to Martha (v. 27)? Jesus had to get Martha to the place where she believed that He had power. Then she was ready for a miracle!

How did Mary enter the scene (vv. 28–33)? Describe her frame of mind. What was she focusing on?

What powers did the Jerusalem Jews think Jesus had (v. 37)? They needed to realize that Jesus was in control and was following God's timing. Just because things hadn't gone as they had hoped didn't mean that His power was diminished.

Sometimes we forget that Jesus walked this earth as a man. We forget that He loved His friends and felt sorrow at their pain. He was sad when His friend died. He hurt when His disciples and friends did not understand His power. He hurt to see the unbelief in the Jews.

Keep in mind the picture of Jesus weeping (v. 35) and remember that He loves you as much as He loved Lazarus.

Now put yourself in the story. If you were in the crowd, what would you have been thinking when Jesus said, "Take away the stone"?

What thought crossed Martha's mind (v. 39)? What tone of voice do you think Jesus used (v. 40)? Describe what it must have been like to see Lazarus come out of the grave!

This story pictures what would be happening to Jesus in just a few months. He probably was thinking about that as He watched His friend. Do you think the tempter ever gave up trying to make Jesus think of an easy way out? What Jesus did for us was extremely hard for Him because He chose to do it in His human strength—even though He had power over death.

This story also pictures what Jesus does for us now. When He calls us to follow Him, we come forth from the power of sin and death, just as Lazarus came forth from the tomb. From that moment on we have His power to say no to the tempter just as Jesus did.

In the last command of the story Jesus told the bystanders to take the grave clothes off Lazarus and let him go free. When Jesus sets us free, nothing else can claim power over us (see John 8:36).

BACK TO SQUARE ONE

Give some thought to Holly's situation.

- List three or four things to say to Holly that will set her at ease.
- Will you advise her to speak to anyone else? If so, whom?
- How do Holly's parents affect this problem?
- What other temptations will she face if she doesn't deal with the second of her two enemies?
- What difference should being a Christian make?
- Lazarus was not the only person affected by the miracle in this story. Those who saw or heard of the power of God were forced to make a choice. Do you believe that God has that kind of power? Think of one example from your own life of God's power that you can tell Holly.
- Holly also needs to know that what Jesus did a few months later on Calvary was because He felt her pain and wanted to provide a way for her to be rid of the pain and the guilt. To say that what He did was enough to pay for every sin—except this one—is to tell Jesus that what He did was not enough! Think of that next time you are tempted to hang on to guilt for a sin that has been forgiven. What could you say to Holly to help her understand the meaning of forgiveness?

MOVING AHEAD

What does it mean to be free? It means you are free to do anything Jesus would do in your situation. For the next few weeks, practice claiming and using your freedom through the power of Jesus.

- Identify one or more things that "bind" you. (Habits you can't break or temptations that get to you frequently.)
- Write in a few words what you would like to be freed from.
- Take them to the Lord and ask to be set free.
- Lazarus could have stayed in his grave clothes, but he didn't want to. Guilt is like grave clothes. Think of Lazarus next time you are tempted. Do you really want to go around wearing grave clothes?
- Share your experience with each other and listen—without judgment—as your partner shares with you.
- Keep a record of your thoughts and experience on the "Keeping Track" page.

QUOTES & STUFF

Justified means that God accepts me *just as if I'd* never sinned.

Many promising reconciliations have broken down because while both parties came prepared to forgive, neither party came to be forgiven. —*Anonymous*

JUST FOR FUN

1. Make this mathematical statement true by adding + and - signs where you need them: 1 2 3 4 5 6 7 8 9 = 2 0 0

2. Using the number 1 through 9 only once each, find a way to make this equation true:

$$\begin{array}{ccc} \underline{\quad} & \underline{\quad} & \underline{\quad} \\ + \quad \underline{\quad} & \underline{\quad} & \underline{\quad} \\ \hline \underline{\quad} & \underline{\quad} & \underline{\quad} \end{array}$$

3. Arrange 10 dimes in 5 rows with 4 in each row.

(Answers appear in chapter 11 "Quotes & Stuff.")

KEEPING TRACK

Teen: _____

_____

_____

_____

_____

_____

_____

Parent: _____

_____

_____

_____

_____

_____

_____

ELEVEN

Who Called Me?

Jesus immediately said to them: "Take
courage! It is I. Don't be afraid."

MATTHEW 4:27

Michael helps out with a boy's club in the downtown area of his city. At first he volunteered just two days a week after school, but within a few months he was spending three afternoons and every Saturday morning with the kids.

Michael loves the sports program he runs, but his favorite thing is the Wednesday afternoon Bible study. No one really expected many boys to be interested, but each Wednesday the little room is full of teens who come because they admire Michael so much. Very few of them have a positive male role model at home, and Michael is honored to show them that even men need a relationship with God to deal with life's problems.

The club director thinks Michael has a real gift for working with children and has encouraged him to consider this kind of work as a career. He even offered Michael a job as assistant director of summer programs. The hours would be long and the pay not so great, but Michael really feels that God is calling him into this kind of work.

Michael plans to go to college in one more year, and he really needs a job that pays well so he can save money for tuition. Although his parents are proud of the work he does

with the boys, they are urging him to take a higher-paying job at the local factory.

Discuss the following:

Choices are much easier to make when one of the options is obviously wrong! In Michael's situation, neither is bad, so he'll have to decide which is better.

- Describe a time when you were in a situation like Michael's and had to choose between two things that both seemed good. What happened? Looking back, do you think you made the right choice? Why or why not?
- Who should have the final say about Michael's decision?
- What alternatives can you think of other than the two obvious choices?
- How should Michael's parents handle this situation?
- What do you think obedience to Jesus is in this problem?

Jesus had a very special friend who was eager to follow Him, but often didn't know how. Throughout his life this friend had to learn to trust and obey Jesus. He had to learn to listen for His voice and follow Him, no matter what.

WHAT'S OUR EXAMPLE?

Take turns reading Matthew 14:22–32.

²²Immediately Jesus made the disciples get into the boat and go on ahead of him to the other side, while he dismissed the crowd. ²³After he had dismissed them, he went up on a mountainside by himself to pray. When evening came, he was there alone, ²⁴but the boat was already a considerable distance from land, buffeted by the waves because the wind was against it.

²⁵During the fourth watch of the night Jesus went out to them, walking on the lake. ²⁶When the disciples saw him walking on the lake, they were terrified. "It's a ghost," they said, and cried out in fear.

²⁷But Jesus immediately said to them: "Take courage! It is I. Don't be afraid."

²⁸"Lord, if it's you," Peter replied, "tell me to come to you on the water."

²⁹"Come," he said.

Then Peter got down out of the boat, walked on the water and came toward Jesus. ³⁰But when he saw the wind, he was afraid and, beginning to sink, cried out, "Lord, save me!"

³¹Immediately Jesus reached out his hand and caught him. "You of little faith," he said, "why did you doubt?" ³²And when they climbed into the boat, the wind died down.

WHAT'S THE ANSWER?

When evening came, Jesus was alone. Earlier that day He had fed 5,000 people with one small lunch. Then He had sent the disciples on ahead without Him. Why (v. 23; John 6:14–15)? The disciples were about three miles out in the lake and were having trouble rowing against the wind. Between 3 and 6 A.M., Jesus walked—on the water—to the spot where the disciples were struggling. Notice the reaction of these twelve grown men (v. 26). Why do you think Jesus did this miracle?

Every day these men were seeing things that they could not explain. They were in a constant state of wonder and awe at the things Jesus was doing and teaching. But they needed to learn that Jesus wasn't doing tricks just to impress them. He was preparing them to be leaders. Before long His physical presence would be removed from them and they would need to know how to claim God's power and to seek God's will on their own. Jesus had the disciples help Him feed all those people the night before because He wanted His friends to realize that God's power was available to them then, and He wanted them to realize the same thing now.

Peter finally caught on! Verses 28–30 are a short story of triumph. Peter actually trusted Jesus enough to step out of the boat in the middle of a lake in the middle of a storm! Wouldn't it be wonderful if the story ended with Jesus and all twelve men abandoning their boat in the middle of the lake and walking to shore? Unfortunately, the ending is quite different (v. 30).

What caused Peter's problem? If he had kept his eyes fixed on Jesus, what do you think the outcome would have been?

Jesus saw His friend fail. A lesser man than Jesus might have dunked Peter once to teach him a lesson, or let him thrash about in the cold water for a while. But see how quickly Jesus responded to Peter's cry, "Lord, save me!" (v. 31).

What lesson do you think the disciples learned from this adventure on the lake? What have you learned about God's power. Is that power available to you? What do you need to do to experience God's power in your life?

When challenges arise in your life, follow these steps:

1. Look for Jesus. You will need Bible study and prayer before you can see where Jesus is leading.
2. Trust. Once you have decided that Jesus is leading in a particular direction, trust Him. Let your doubts go.
3. Step out. Take some steps toward your goal.
4. Keep your eyes on Jesus. Once you are on your way, don't change your focal point! Obstacles and alternatives will only distract you from your goal of reaching Jesus.
5. If you find yourself in trouble, turn back to Jesus for help immediately. There is no shame in having trouble, but there is shame in shifting your trust to yourself and your own abilities.

BACK TO SQUARE ONE

Give some thought to Michael's situation.

- Michael is facing a decision that only he can make. What can you say or do to make the decision easier for him?
- Michael will probably be getting advice from all sides and every angle! There are some practical things to think about. There are some matters of conviction to think about. If you were Michael, how would you go about sorting through the options?
- What should be Michael's ultimate goal?
- What do you think Peter would tell Michael about stepping out on faith? What would Peter have missed if he had never tried?
- What would Jesus say to Michael?

MOVING AHEAD

- What was Peter's challenge to Jesus?
- What was Jesus' challenge to Peter?
- Identify one area of your life in which you think the Lord might be calling you to do something special.
- Write a plan of action using the five steps on page 141.
- List some ways to help each other act on these challenges.
- Keep a record of your thoughts and experiences on the "Keeping Track" page.

QUOTES & STUFF

He is most fatigued who knows not what to do. —*N. Beileau*

Don't dig up in doubt what you've planted in faith. Go ahead and do the thing, pay the price, carry through and finish it. Never mind Satan's attacks. —*Elisabeth Elliot*

You can do more than pray, after you have prayed. But you can not do more than pray until you have prayed. —*S. D. Gordon*

JUST FOR FUN

It's the law! Really!

• Barbers in Waterloo, Nebraska, are forbidden to eat onions between 7 A.M. and 7 P.M.

• A Chicago law forbids eating in a place that is on fire.

• In Hillsboro, Oregon, it is unlawful to allow a horse to ride around in the back seat of your car.
—from *Crazy Laws by Dick Hyman*

Answers to puzzle in chapter 10.

1. 123 + 4 + 5 + 67 -8 +9 = 200   3. Draw a 5-pointed star and put
2. 357 + 624 = 981   a dime wherever lines intersect.

KEEPING TRACK

Teen: _____

_____

_____

_____

_____

_____

Parent: _____

_____

_____

_____

_____

_____

TWELVE

He Can't Bug Me If He Can't Find Me

Give to everyone who asks you, and if
anyone takes what belongs to you, do
not demand it back. Do to others as you
would have them do to you.

LUKE 6:30–31

John and Sharon Milikin live in a nice house in a nice neighborhood. They have nicely trimmed bushes and well-planned gardens that bloom most of the year. John and Sharon are very proud of their home.

John has been buying tools every time he gets a little extra spending money. He keeps them hanging neatly and in order in the workshop he has in his garage.

Across the street from the Milikins lives a single man named Oscar. Oscar makes a rather marginal attempt at keeping up his property, but he too likes tools—especially John's tools. Last year he borrowed several small gardening tools that John never saw again. Just last week Oscar returned John's shovel in two pieces and suggested that he complain to the hardware store about the quality of items they sell. He backed over John's garden hose and lost the bits to John's drill.

John never goes into the front yard anymore without first looking out the window to see if Oscar is there.

Oscar is a loner. No family or friends ever come to visit him. John would like Oscar to disappear. Sharon says that John should be more friendly to Oscar and maybe even invite him over to watch a game on T.V. sometime. "Maybe he would come to church with us if we made him feel comfortable.

Finding the Lord could be just what Oscar needs," she said. "Maybe then he'd return some of your stuff."

John says he would rather eat sawdust than ask Oscar into his home.

Discuss the following:

- Describe a time when you had to deal with someone like Oscar. How did you feel about the situation?
- Do either John or Sharon have the right response? Explain.
- How do you think Sharon would respond if Oscar had a wife who borrowed all of her things? Or if Oscar had a child who broke all of her child's toys?
- What options do you have as a Christian?

The Bible doesn't identify any Oscars, but Jesus did teach a lesson about how to deal with people who make our lives miserable. This is a lesson we already know, but we need to hear it over and over because most of us would rather forget it.

WHAT'S OUR EXAMPLE?

Take turns reading Luke 6:27–36.

27"But I tell you who hear me: Love your enemies, do good to those who hate you, 28bless those who curse you, pray for those who mistreat you. 29If someone strikes you on one cheek, turn to him the other also. If someone takes your cloak, do not stop him from taking your tunic. 30Give to everyone who asks you, and if anyone takes what belongs to you, do not demand it back. 31Do to others as you would have them do to you.

³²"If you love those who love you, what credit is that to you? Even 'sinners' love those who love them. ³³And if you do good to those who are good to you, what credit is that to you? Even 'sinners' do that. ³⁴And if you lend to those from whom you expect repayment, what credit is that to you? Even 'sinners' lend to 'sinners,' expecting to be repaid in full. ³⁵But love your enemies, do good to them, and lend to them without expecting to get anything back. Then your reward will be great, and you will be sons of the Most High, because he is kind to the ungrateful and wicked. ³⁶Be merciful, just as your Father is merciful."

WHAT'S THE ANSWER?

We call verse 31 the Golden Rule. People quote it often because it is good advice. However, when most people use it they neglect to include the four verses that precede it. To them it is a principle to use when dealing with somebody they already like or someone they may never see again.

Read the first five verses again and discuss what kind of people are mentioned. When you are mistreated, what should be your first response? Be honest! How are we to do what verse 28 says? Are we to let people walk all over us? What about self-defense? When, if ever, is it all right to strike back? Maybe a good paraphrase of the Golden Rule would be "Do unto others as Jesus would do unto them." Is that possible?

The disciples were listening to this sermon, and Jesus was directing His words to them, knowing what kind of things awaited them in the coming years. For them following Jesus would mean constant persecution and, for all but one of them, a martyr's death. If the world was to see Christ in them and be changed, the disciples would have to live Christlike lives even in the worst situations. Following Jesus would require the toughest kind of self-control. The only possible way to obey this is in love, and the only love great enough to overcome the temptation to retaliate is Christ's love. It is as difficult to follow this simple little Golden Rule as it is to walk on water, and it requires the same power. We must keep our eyes focused on Jesus and remember how much He loves that unlovable person.

We must also recognize that thoughts of gratification through revenge come from the tempter. Satan is always looking for ways to score a little victory—to enjoy a little control over God's children.

Verses 32–38 explain God's standards. He has not called us to be like everybody else. He expects us to be like our heavenly Father. For this we need a power much greater than self-control. When we begin to act and think in ways that remind others of our Father, we are under the control of the Holy Spirit.

When we are calmly studying our Bibles it is easy to convince ourselves that we will react in a godly way in an ugly situation. But thinking about being good and actually being good are not the same, and when an ugly situation arises we often fail the test. Why is this?

Study the passage to find the reward Jesus mentions. What is it? Is it worth the hassle?

BACK TO SQUARE ONE

Give some thought to John's situation.

The most difficult battles to fight are those against an enemy in disguise. Perhaps you can help John see that his situation is full of temptation.

• List some of those temptations.

• With this in mind, what advice do you have for John?

• What about Sharon? How do you think she would respond if Oscar did go to church with them but still didn't return the things he had taken? Does Jesus address the issue of lending? How does what He said apply to people like Oscar?

• What steps could John take that would be consistent with his Christian life but would prohibit Oscar from showing such disrespect toward him and his things?

• If Jesus lived across the street, how would He treat Oscar?

MOVING AHEAD

- Tell each other about one experience you had when you were in an ugly situation and behaved consistently with today's Scripture. What was the outcome? How did you feel? Look upon that experience as evidence of what the Holy Spirit can do when you yield control to Him.
- With your new understanding of this command, try for the next few weeks to bless truly awful people. You need to show Christ's love when someone who hates you tries to make you angry.
- Think of this effort as facing the devil himself. Pray that God will control your temper and allow you to see through the eyes of Jesus. Recognize Satan in situations that tempt you to abandon Christ's love. Spend time in prayer and arm yourself with ammunition for the fight. Listen to Christian music and talk to God a lot so you will be ready to face an ugly situation. You can be sure the devil will see your preparation as a challenge, and you will have a battle.
- Be prepared to discuss the experiences you have and tell what obedience to Jesus means to you.
- Keep a record of your thoughts and experiences on the "Keeping Track" page.

Go for it! The victory will be so sweet!

QUOTES & STUFF

A Christian's life is the world's Bible. —*D. L. Moody*

Rudeness is a weak person's imitation of strength.

Words are like medicine: measure them with care; an overdose can hurt. —*Leo Rosten's Treasury of Jewish Quotations*

Be kind and compassionate to one another, forgiving each other, just as in Christ God forgave you. —*Ephesians 4:32*

JUST FOR FUN

Only one ten-letter word can be written by using just the top row of letter keys on a typewriter. The word is *typewriter*.

You have to count all the way to one thousand before the letter *a* is used in spelling a number.

There are only twelve letters in the Hawaiian alphabet: a, e, h, i k, l m, n, o, p, u, w.

KEEPING TRACK

Teen: _____

_____

_____

_____

_____

_____

_____

Parent: _____

_____

_____

_____

_____

_____

_____

Note to the Reader

The publisher invites you to share your response to the message of this book by writing Discovery House Publishers, P. O. Box 3566, Grand Rapids, MI 49501, U.S.A. or by calling 1-800-283-8333. For information about other Discovery House publications, contact us at the same address and phone number.